E-SPORTS GAME ON!

Cheating in E-Sports

by Marcia Amidon Lusted

NORWOOD HOUSE PRESS

Norwood House Press
P.O. Box 316598
Chicago, Illinois 60631

For information regarding Norwood House Press, please visit our website at:
www.norwoodhousepress.com or call 866-565-2900.

Content Consultant: Phill Alexander, assistant professor of games, Armstrong Institute for Interactive Media Studies, Miami University, Ohio

LIBRARY OF CONGRESS CATALOGING-IN-PUBLICATION DATA

Names: Lusted, Marcia Amidon, author.
Title: Cheating in E-sports / by Marcia Amidon Lusted.
Description: Chicago, Illinois : Norwood House Press, 2018. | Series:
    E-sports : game on! | Includes bibliographical references and index.
Identifiers: LCCN 2018004327 (print) | LCCN 2018003217 (ebook) | ISBN
    9781684042623 (ebook) | ISBN 9781599539638 (hardcover : alk. paper)
Subjects: LCSH: Cheating at video games--Juvenile literature.
Classification: LCC GV1469.34.C67 (print) | LCC GV1469.34.C67 L87 2018
    (ebook) | DDC 794.8--dc23
LC record available at https://lccn.loc.gov/2018004327

312N—072018
Manufactured in the United States of America in North Mankato, Minnesota.

CONTENTS

Chapter 1:
Welcome to E-Sports   4

Chapter 2:
Why They Cheat   13

Chapter 3:
How They Cheat   21

Chapter 4:
Stopping the Cheaters   33

Glossary   44

For More Information   45

Index   46

About the Author   48

Note: Words that are **bolded** in the text are defined in the glossary.

Welcome to E-Sports

The **arena** is packed with screaming, cheering fans. They wear shirts from their favorite teams. Colored spotlights sweep over the crowd. Above the noise, the emcee yells. He asks the **spectators** to make even more noise. Music blares, and giant screens flash with bright colors.

The building frenzy of excitement sounds like any sporting event. But there is no field or court filled with athletes. Instead, the fans are watching 90 competitors sitting on a stage. Each competitor is staring at a small screen. This is The International, the *Dota 2* championship. This video game tournament awarded prizes totaling more than $24.7 million in 2017.

Dota 2 is a multiplayer online battle arena (MOBA) game published by Valve Corporation. It is played by two teams

Players compete at The International, an E-Sports tournament that offers some of the highest amounts of prize money to its participants.

of five players each. The International has players from all over the world. *Dota 2* is popular among players and fans alike, and The International has the most prize money of any E-Sports tournament in the world.

The Rise of E-Sports

E-Sports is professional, competitive video gaming. It is getting more and more popular. By 2017, there were approximately 148 million E-Sports fans all over the world. Approximately 22 percent of young men in the United States watch E-Sports, according to a 2016 survey. That means watching E-Sports is as popular as watching baseball or hockey.

Most E-Sports fans watch online using websites such as Twitch and YouTube Gaming.

DID YOU KNOW?

Typically, between 400,000 and 700,000 people are playing *Dota 2* at any given time. The record for the most people playing at the same time is 1.3 million.

What Is *Dota 2*?

The original game of *Dota*, which stands for *Defense of the Ancients*, was a multiplayer online game in which two teams battled each other. *Dota* was a fan-created modification of the game *Warcraft III*. In 2013, Valve Corporation released *Dota 2*, separate from the fan-created *Dota*. In *Dota 2*, teams battle each other, similar to the original *Dota*. Players can choose from 100 possible hero characters. *Dota 2* is free to play. It has millions of dedicated players.

A fan watches a *Dota 2* match online at Twitch.tv. Twitch is the most popular website for watching E-Sports.

Unlike traditional sports broadcasts on TV, video streams on these websites allow viewers to interact with players and broadcasters in real time. E-Sports competitions and tournaments sell out huge sporting venues. Events have been held at Madison Square Garden in New York City and at the Staples Center in Los Angeles, California.

Fans cheer at a *Counter-Strike: Global Offensive* tournament in Russia in 2017. E-Sports tournaments have sold out arenas all over the world.

Making Money

E-Sports isn't just for fans to watch. It has also become something that fans bet on. E-Sports gamblers can gamble with real money. However, they usually gamble using "skins." Skins are virtual items that players can win in a game. Skins are often used to change the appearance of characters, weapons,

Skins

Skins can be used to change the appearance or characteristics of characters or weapons in video games. Skins are often used for gambling, but they started out as just a way for players to customize their games. Many players feel that special skins make their characters or weapons elite. This is especially important when other players are watching. It shows a dedication to the game.

and equipment within a game. But skins can also be traded or used for placing bets. In some cases, skins can even be cashed out for real money. This is usually done between players and not as an official part of a game. Using skins to gamble has become increasingly popular. Players gambled more than $7 billion worth of skins in 2016.

Cheating to Win

Because of the huge amounts of money available for players and gamblers, cheating is becoming more common in E-Sports. Cheating is wrong. In E-Sports, cheating can lead to public shame and disqualification from tournaments. People who have been disqualified because of cheating do not get to keep

DID YOU KNOW?

In 2014, 27 million people watched the *League of Legends* world championship. That's more than the number of people that watched each game of baseball's World Series. It is the same number of viewers as the college basketball national championships.

An E-Sports player carries a trophy his team won at a tournament in Russia. The large prize amounts that come with winning E-Sports tournaments have become a motivation for some players to cheat.

their prize money. But as E-Sports prize amounts increase, the potential rewards for cheating grow. Some people are willing to take the serious risks associated with cheating because they want money. Gambling in E-Sports isn't regulated by law like it is for many traditional sports. This can make it seem easy to cheat in E-Sports.

So far, E-Sports leagues and teams have relied on self-policing. They try to prevent cheating by using their own punishments. They may **ban** players from games or publicly shame them. When a player is publicly shamed, his or her name is posted online. This allows other people to make negative comments about that player. But these kinds of punishments aren't stopping serious gamblers and players from finding ways to cheat. Understanding cheating in E-Sports means understanding why the cheating happens, how it happens, and how people are trying to stop it.

As E-Sports have become more popular, cheating has increased at all levels of competition.

CHAPTER 2

Why They Cheat

I f E-Sports competitions were just for fun, then perhaps cheating wouldn't be important to anyone but the players. However, E-Sports tournaments offer prize money to their winners. And the amount of money for these prizes is growing. This makes more people willing to cheat to get that money.

Money, Money, Money

In 2017, The International had the largest combined prize pool of any professional E-Sports tournament on record, according to the website E-Sports Earnings. The prizes totaled about $24.7 million. The next-highest prize on record was The International 2016, which had a combined prize pool of about $20.7 million. And those are just the top tournament prizes. The lowest-earning tournament out of the 500 events tracked by E-Sports Earnings still offered prizes totaling $100,000. Ian Smith, head of the Esports Integrity Coalition (ESIC), said E-Sports players can "go from playing in their parents' basement to playing in a $5 million tournament in six months." Naturally, the growth of cheating has followed the popularity of E-Sports.

Cheating to Lose

E-Sports players may win with cheating **tactics** such as **hacking** or performance-boosting drugs. But cheating in E-Sports isn't simply about cheating to win a competition and collect a large prize. Some players actually cheat to lose, which is called **match fixing**. In match fixing, players may be paid large amounts of money to play poorly and lose their match, letting another player win. This kind of cheating

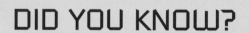

DID YOU KNOW?

After a high-ranking *Counter-Strike: Global Offensive* player admitted that he and his teammates used Adderall to win tournaments, the Electronic Sports League (ESL) started a program for drug testing all tournament players.

Tournament Drugs

Many E-Sports organizations are cracking down on the use of performance-enhancing drugs. One drug commonly used by E-Sports players is Adderall. It is usually prescribed for attention deficit hyperactivity disorder (ADHD) and narcolepsy, a sleep disorder that causes people to fall asleep unexpectedly. Adderall also has the side effect of increasing alertness and reaction times. That side effect can be attractive to people playing games. Split-second reflexes can make the difference between winning and losing a tournament.

has happened in many professional sports, such as football and boxing, for years.

Match fixing can be difficult to notice in E-Sports. T.K. Park, an expert

DID YOU KNOW?

In 2015, Pakistani player Sumail Hassan Syed, known by his gaming name "Suma1L," became the youngest player to win $1 million in a *Dota 2* tournament. He was 16 years, 2 months, and 21 days old.

on the Korean E-Sports industry, has said, "It would not be super obvious to the spectators—a player can simply

In many E-Sports games, even a split-second delay can allow one player to overtake another.

do everything just a fraction of a second slower and that will be enough to throw a game." Fixing can also involve gambling with skins. Players can bet against themselves with skins and then lose on purpose. This can bring them more money than they would earn by actually winning the game.

DID YOU KNOW?

On average, E-Sports players are between 24 and 27 years old.

Match fixing in E-Sports doesn't just affect the winners and losers. It can have a significant impact on the reputation of the E-Sports industry itself. This happened in South Korea in 2010. The E-Sports game *StarCraft* was extremely popular there. Then eight players were found guilty of match fixing and gambling in *StarCraft*. The group included South Korea's most famous player at the time. As a result of the scandal, E-Sports' popularity in South Korea fell overnight. The E-Sports industry lost credibility. In another case, a Russian *Dota 2* player was given a lifetime ban from playing in tournaments. He bet against his own team and then gave a suspiciously poor performance in a match.

Although prize money can encourage competition at E-Sports tournaments, many players want to win regardless of prizes. They just want to show that they are the best.

Splitting the Pot, Losing the Game

During the Major League Gaming (MLG) summer championships in 2012, the first- and second-place teams playing *League of Legends* were both disqualified and stripped of their winnings. The MLG determined that the two teams had conspired to split the prize money from their final match. One of the teams may have agreed to intentionally lose. MLG executive Adam Apicella said that the teams had made the agreement "in a public, crowded setting" in front of witnesses. "The entire venue was aware of it," he said. The teams did not contest the ruling to disqualify them. The third- and fourth-place teams were awarded the prize money instead.

Another form of cheating benefits both teams playing in a match. It is unfair to the fans who hope for games with healthy competition and tension. It is called "splitting the pot." Two friendly teams facing each other decide before the game that they will split the prize money, no matter who actually wins. These kinds of pregame arrangements are not strictly called match fixing, but they are against the spirit of the games. Teams that have been caught making

The Cinderella Law

South Korea was one of the first centers for E-Sports, and the popularity of computer gaming there is very high. However, the South Korean government became concerned about the high rates of computer game addiction among young people. As a result, the government implemented the Shutdown Law, also called the Cinderella Law, in 2011. This shuts down access to gaming sites between midnight and 6:00 a.m. for anyone under the age of 16. The law has been very controversial. It has been amended to allow parents to decide when gaming should take place in their homes.

these kinds of deals have had their prize money stripped from them.

For the Glory

People also cheat in E-Sports simply because they want to win games and become popular in the gaming world. It is the same competitiveness that makes players in any sport want to win games and break records. This drive to win leads some players to cheat.

CHAPTER 3

How They Cheat

The tournament for *Counter-Strike: Global Offensive* is in full swing. The audience fills the auditorium. They are excited and enthusiastic. With every shot that a player makes, the audience roars with approval. The atmosphere is fun and energetic. But this atmosphere can also be a way for players to cheat.

The players are in soundproof booths. They can't hear or see what their opponents are doing. They move through the game, unable to tell where an opponent may be hiding. But the noise of the crowd can create another kind of cheating situation. Players can feel the vibrations from the crowd noise, even when they're in soundproof booths. The audience will cheer when a player gets close to an opponent who is hiding. The player may not be able to see the hidden opponent, but the crowd's noise can help the player guess where the opponent is. Using audience noise may not be outright cheating in a tournament, but it can give players an **advantage**.

Players can also use specifically timed Internet outages to change the outcome of a game. By getting a group of hackers to interrupt an Internet connection, even for a moment, a player can cause his or her opponents to lose valuable playing time. The player who organizes the outage can use that time to get ahead in the game.

Hacks to Win

Because E-Sports are entirely based on computer gaming, it's not surprising that many of the ways that players can cheat involve hacking. This includes players hacking the games themselves or using external software that modifies the games. Some hacking tools are easy for any gamer to use. Others require cheaters to have more extensive computer-programming knowledge. Hacking takes place at all levels of gaming, from amateur players at home to pros participating in high-level professional tournaments.

E-Sports players often practice or compete in enclosed booths.

There are many hacks that players use to cheat. One type is a "wall hack." A wall hack shows the outlines of opponents anywhere on the game's map, even through

Computer-programming knowledge is needed for some E-Sports cheating hacks.

walls. This lets players aim at their opponents without being seen.

There are also hacks that can enhance players' skills. For example, some hacks can

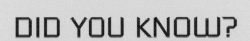

make players better at shooting. An aimbot hack automatically targets an opponent when the opponent approaches. The player doesn't even need to be looking at opponents in order for the aimbot to target them. Aimbots can also target several enemies very quickly, enabling the player to wipe out a whole team in seconds. Another hack, auto triggering, makes the player's weapon automatically fire a stream of bullets every time it sees a clear shot at the opponent's head, even when the opponent is concealed by a wall. Hacks can also include a teleportation feature that automatically places the player's character in the best

Cheating or Not?

In 2016, a well-known gamer was supposedly caught cheating at the video game *Tom Clancy's Rainbow Six Siege*. This game has a smaller following than many others, but it was growing in popularity at the time. The game awarded cash prizes for winners of its weekly and monthly competitions. A group of players released video that seemed to show the well-known gamer using a second screen and glancing over at it while playing. This is forbidden in professional matches because it can give away the location of other players. The suspected cheater stated that he works in the computer industry and that he was simply glancing over at the second monitor for work reasons, but he has since stepped down from professional play.

place to start a match, before the opponents can get out of the way.

Hackers may use external software programs that aren't approved by the game's manufacturer. Sometimes this software isn't strictly illegal, but it violates the gaming software's terms of service. Some of these software programs enable players to dodge enemy players' attacks in ways that aren't allowed within the game. Other software programs enable players to accumulate resources such as

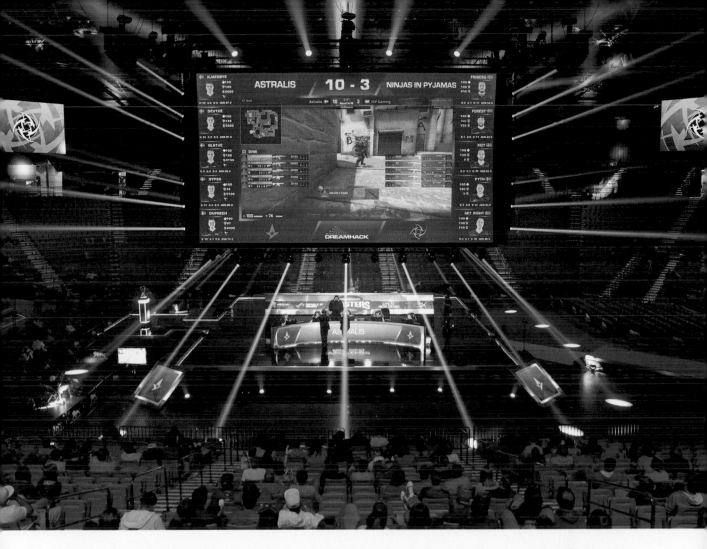

Wall hacks are popular in the game *Counter-Strike*. *Counter-Strike* is popular at major E-Sports tournaments.

gold or weapons quickly so they can advance through the game faster.

Cheating with software is a major problem for the E-Sports industry. Companies such as ESL, which organizes E-Sports tournaments, pay online spies to get cheating software so they can study these programs. They want to figure out how to prevent players from using them. Gaming companies and E-Sports organizations are also banning players who are caught using cheating software.

Who Are You?

Players can also cheat by using fake accounts. Experienced players with high skill ratings will create "smurf accounts." These are new accounts designed to make other players think that the player is new and inexperienced. Players with less experience will play against the smurf, thinking that the smurf is new to the game. The smurf then dominates

DID YOU KNOW?

The term "smurfing" supposedly comes from two experienced *Warcraft II* players. When they found that no one would play against them, they created new accounts, calling themselves "Papa Smurf" and "Smurfette," after the television cartoon characters.

Sometimes E-Sports players work together to cheat. Other times, a player hurts his or her own team by getting caught cheating.

the opponent because he or she is actually very skilled. Smurfing can help players score an easy win. Smurfing takes place among both amateur and professional players, in all levels of tournaments.

A fake profile also helps a gamer keep playing after being banned from a game for cheating. There are also software hacks that will continually change the profile name

A gaming mouse functions differently than a regular computer mouse.

of a player during a game. This creates confusion and annoyance for the other players.

The Cheating Mouse

Players can also cheat using their computer hardware itself. Most hardware cheats are done by professional players in high-stakes tournaments. Even during high-profile tournaments, players are often allowed to bring their own keyboards and mice. Many players have sponsorship deals with computer hardware makers. As part of these deals, they have to play tournaments using their sponsors' equipment.

A mouse used for gaming is not like a regular computer mouse. These mice are essentially tiny computers in themselves. They contain tiny **microprocessors** that enable them to be fast and precise. They contain memory to allow them to easily be used with different computers. However, researchers have discovered that a gaming mouse can be taken apart and modified to accept the code for a cheating program. The resulting hacks may be small, such as a tiny adjustment in how a gun aims at an opponent, but they are enough to make a difference in a game.

Cheating in E-Sports isn't just about friendly competition and achieving a good ranking. Cheaters are often also trying to win a large amount of money. Cheating damages the reputation of E-Sports in general, and it could affect the future of the industry. For this reason, the E-Sports community has started to address cheating more aggressively than ever before.

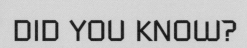

DID YOU KNOW?

Panopticon Laboratories, a cybersecurity company, estimates that players around the world spend between $350 million and $500 million on cheat software every year.

CHAPTER 4

Stopping the Cheaters

E-Sports is still a new form of competitive sports. It is not as established as mainstream sports like football or baseball. Confronting the issue of cheating is vital to E-Sports becoming widely accepted.

Chasing Cheaters

The E-Sports industry is working hard to find ways to fight cheating. One of these is the Valve Anti-Cheat system, or VAC. It was developed by the Valve Corporation as part of its Steam gaming platform. The VAC is an automated system designed to detect cheats on a player's gaming system. VAC automatically bans players who are caught connecting to a VAC-secured server from a computer with verified cheats installed on it. Those bans stop users from playing games on any VAC-secured servers in the future. The VAC system finds cheats based on the signatures they

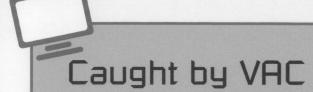

Caught by VAC

In 2014, VAC caught three players cheating. The players, who were from different teams, were headed to a *Counter-Strike: Global Offensive* tournament in Sweden. They were kicked out of the tournament. They also received lifetime bans from any future competitions. The results of the ban affected not only the players but also their teams and sponsors.

DID YOU KNOW?

The VAC system has banned more than 2 million Steam accounts since it was implemented in 2002.

leave on a computer. Cheats or hacks, such as third-party software designed to give gamers an advantage, will trigger a VAC ban. VAC bans are permanent, can't be negotiated, and can't be removed by Steam's support system.

However, the Esports Integrity Coalition has stated that VAC bans are often arbitrary and unfair. The coalition said that a young teenager downloading an aimbot should not be

As the popularity of E-Sports increases, E-Sports industry leaders are working to find better ways to stop cheaters.

A gamer uses a Steam controller to choose a game. Steam is the most popular computer gaming platform.

punished as seriously as a professional E-Sports competitor cheating to win thousands of dollars. The coalition also said the E-Sports industry needs clear and concise rules and procedures for dealing with cheating across all games and platforms, including appropriate punishments. It also said players should be able to appeal lifetime bans.

Using Hardware

Gaming organizations and tournaments are also turning to hardware solutions for detecting and preventing cheating. Most live tournaments take place using LANs, or local area networks. These are networks that connect computers and other

DID YOU KNOW?

The Steam software platform is the largest digital distribution platform for computer gaming. With 150 million registered accounts, it controls a majority of the gaming market. Some games require Steam access, but many players use Steam for all of their games simply out of convenience.

devices within a small area, such as an arena or a single building. The E-Sports Entertainment Association League (ESEA) has developed a special type of anticheating software for use in LAN situations such as tournaments.

These professional gamers are using a LAN, or local area network. The E-Sports Entertainment Association has developed software to stop cheating on LANs during tournaments.

The system lets tournament organizers make sure that players aren't receiving any online help from outside sources.

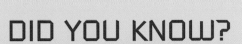
Manufacturers are also creating devices with built-in anticheating protections. One device, called Game:ref, connects to the computer, the mouse, and the Internet. It can see if the mouse's movements match what is happening on the computer. If they don't match, then it is likely that the player is cheating.

It is already difficult to cheat on **console** games because anticheating solutions are built into their software. Many E-Sports industry experts believe that the same cheat preventions need to be built into personal computers to

States and E-Sports Gambling

It can be difficult for states to make laws that regulate E-Sports gambling. This is partly because the E-Sports industry is still developing, which makes E-Sports difficult to define. However, Nevada has a law called Regulation 22 that allows organizations with sports-betting licenses to also accept bets on "other events." If an event, such as a single E-Sports gaming tournament, is approved by the Nevada Gaming Control Board, then the event's license holder can take bets on that event. This allows gambling on E-Sports events to be controlled. In most states, however, betting on E-Sports is not legal or regulated by law.

limit their vulnerability to cheating. Another option is to control access to equipment and make sure that it has not been tampered with. Riot Games, a video game developer and E-Sports tournament organizer, has started requiring professional players in its *League of Legends* competitions to keep unopened sets of equipment at Riot Games' facility so that no cheat software can be installed before a match.

Other Ways to Control Cheating

Despite these existing methods to control cheating, some in the E-Sports industry believe that a formal organization should be created to help. This group would govern E-Sports and enforce anticheating and gambling rules.

States and the federal government are beginning to regulate gambling in E-Sports. E-Sports gamblers can

Some professional E-Sports tournaments have restrictions on the equipment gamers use. These restrictions are to make sure players can't tamper with the hardware to cheat.

The E-Sports industry is still changing as competitive video gaming becomes more and more popular. Some E-Sports industry leaders want to create a formal group to stop cheating.

avoid federal gambling laws because they use skins instead of money. Members of Congress are working to reform these laws to hold E-Sports gamblers **accountable** to existing gambling laws. Many states are beginning to work on legislation that addresses gambling and cheating in E-Sports.

E-Sports are exciting to play and to watch. They bring people together for fun and competition. But, like any sport, they have become an area where cheating and gambling can flourish. The E-Sports industry is not yet tightly regulated. If E-Sports wants to continue to grow in popularity and be taken seriously, then the industry will have to work hard to make sure that the games are fair and fun.

accountable

When a person or organization is expected to justify its decisions or actions.

advantage

Something that makes one person more likely to succeed than another.

arena

A level area surrounded by seats for spectators where events such as sports take place.

ban

To officially or legally prohibit something or someone.

console

An electronic system that connects to a display and is used to play video games.

hacking

Using a computer to make unauthorized changes to a system.

match fixing

A dishonest activity to make sure that one team wins in a game or sport.

microprocessors

Devices in computers that perform calculations and carry out instructions.

spectators

People who watch a show, game, or other event.

tactics

Strategic actions used to achieve something.

Books

Edwards, Sue Bradford. *Professional Gaming Careers*. Chicago, IL: Norwood House Press, 2018.

Hansen, Dustin. *Game On! Video Game History from Pong and Pac-Man to Mario, Minecraft, and More*. New York, NY: Feiwel & Friends, 2016.

Li, Roland. *Good Luck Have Fun: The Rise of eSports*. New York, NY: Skyhorse Publishing, 2017.

Mooney, Carla. *Inside the E-Sports Industry*. Chicago, IL: Norwood House Press, 2018.

Websites

Esports Kids

https://www.esportskids.com

Super League Gaming

https://champs.superleague.com

A

Adderall, 14, 15

B

banning cheaters, 12, 17, 19, 28, 30, 33–37

C

cheating software, 22–24, 26–28, 31–32, 34
Cinderella Law, 20
Counter-Strike: Global Offensive, 14, 21, 25, 34

D

Dota 2, 4–6, 15, 17

E

Esports Integrity Coalition, 14, 34–37

F

fake online profiles, 28–31

G

gambling, 9, 11, 15, 17, 40–41, 43
gambling laws, 40–41, 43

H

hacking, 14, 22–28, 31–32, 34
hardware cheats, 31–32

I

International, The, 4–5, 13

L

League of Legends, 10, 19, 40
local area networks, 37–38
Los Angeles, California, 7

M

match fixing, 14–20
multiplayer online battle arena games, 4

N
Nevada, 40
New York City, 7

P
publicly shaming cheaters, 10, 12

R
Riot Games, 39–40

S
skins, 9–10, 16, 17, 43
soundproof booths, 21–22
South Korea, 16–17, 20
StarCraft, 16–17
Steam gaming platform, 33–34, 37

T
Tom Clancy's Rainbow Six Siege, 26
Twitch, 6

V
Valve Anti-Cheat, 33–37
Valve Corporation, 4, 6, 33

Y
YouTube Gaming, 6

Marcia Amidon Lusted has written 160 books and more than 600 magazine articles for young readers. She is also a musician and editor and has traveled all over the world.